Sitting Bull

Bravery

The Story of Sitting Bull

by

Perter Murray

Illustrated by

Robin Lawrie

The Child's World®

Library of Congress Cataloging-in-Publication Data
Murray, Peter, 1952 Sept 29-.
Sitting Bull: a story of bravery / Peter Murray.
p. cm.

ISBN 1-56766-230-7

1. Sitting Bull, 1834-1890--Juvenile literature.
2. Dakota Indians--Juvenile literature.
3. Hunkpapa Indians--Biography. 4. Hunkpapa Indians--Kings and rulers. 5.
Hunkpapa Indians--History. I. Title
E99.D1S6125 1996
978, 004975'0092--dc20
[B]
95-42267
CIP
AC

Contents

A Boy Named Slow

One cold March day in 1831, a baby was born in a teepee on the banks of the Grand River. The young mother's name was Her-Holy-Door. The proud father was called Tatanka-Tyotanka. They were Hunkpapa Indians, one of the tribes of the great Sioux nation.

"What shall we name him?" Her-Holy-Door wondered.

"His name will come to us when the time is right," said Tatanka-Tyotanka.

At first, their son was like babies everywhere. He slept. He drank his mother's milk. He gurgled and cooed.

But he was not allowed to cry. The Hunkpapas had many enemies, and a crying baby could bring danger to them all.

Months passed. Soon the baby was eating solid food. He would take a piece of buffalo meat in his tiny hand and look at it carefully. If he liked what he saw, he would eat it.

"Look at your son," said Her-Holy-Door. "He thinks about every bitc."

Tatanka-Tyotanka watched his young son examine a juicy red berry, then pop it into his mouth. "He is slow to act," he said. "I hope he is not slow in the head."

Her-Holy-Door frowned. "Do not say that," she said. "Our son will grow up to be strong, wise, generous, and brave!"

"I hope you are right," said Tatanka-Tyotanka.

The Four Sioux Virtues

The Sioux peoples prized four qualities in their men. A good man showed himself to be wise, generous, strong-hearted, and brave. *Bravery* was considered the most important of the four virtues.

The child grew quickly. Soon, he was playing with the other children in the village of teepees. He was an intelligent and thoughtful child, but the other members of the tribe thought he was slow to act. He liked to think about things before he decided what to do. When he decided what he wanted, he was as stubborn as a bull buffalo. Some of the other children gave him the nickname *Slow*.

Tatanka-Tyotanka was not pleased with his son's nickname, but he said nothing. If the boy was slow to act, then he would be called Slow.

Slow grew older. His father taught him to shoot a bow and ride a pony. He became one of the fastest runners in the tribe. At ten years old he could easily outrun larger and older children, but the name he had been given as a small child stayed with him. They still called him Slow.

What is *Bravery?*

To be brave means to show great courage. In battle, it means that even if you are afraid, you continue to fight. To the Sioux peoples, bravery was the most important quality in a warrior. Without bravery, a man's other qualities meant nothing.

The Young Warrior

In the 1800s, the Hunkpapa people lived by following the buffalo herds across the prairie. Buffalo provided the tribes with meat, skins for their teepees and clothing, and bone for making tools. Buffalo tendons and sinews were used to make rope and to stitch moccasins. Dried buffalo droppings were burned for cooking fires.

Hunting buffalo was a difficult and dangerous job. A group of Hunkpapa men would sneak up on a herd of buffalo, then leap onto their horses and charge, shooting arrows as they rode at top speed across the prairie. They were expert horsemen. Hunkpapa children were taught to ride at an early age. They depended on their horses to hunt the buffalo. The number of horses a family owned showed how rich and important they were.

It was considered an honorable thing for the Hunkpapa men to form raiding parties to steal horses from their enemies, the Crows and the Blackfeet. These raids added to the wealth and the strength of the tribe. They were also an opportunity for the men to show their bravery.

Slow was 14 years old when he went on his first raid. Riding a gray pony and carrying a red coup stick, he followed a small war party into territory controlled by the Crow. They hoped to capture Crow horses and to prove their strength and bravery by fighting their Crow enemies.

One day they spied a Crow camp on the other side of a hill. The Hunkpapa warriors climbed down from their horses and slowly approached the camp, trying to decide how to attack.

Counting Coup

Among the Sioux peoples, the greatest glory came to the warrior who first touched an enemy in battle. By first striking an enemy without killing him, the warrior showed his courage and skill. This was called "counting coup." Only the bravest and most daring warriors counted first coup, and many who tried were killed.

To the amazement of the other Hunkpapas, Slow suddenly leapt on his pony and charged over the hilltop, waving his coup stick and shouting a war cry. The Crows jumped on their horses and fled, but Slow's gray pony was faster. He caught up with one of the Crow warriors and knocked him from his horse, counting first coup.

The battle lasted only a few minutes, and when it was over, all but four of the Crow were dead. The raiding party returned in triumph to the Hunkpapa village, where the story of Slow's brave charge was told again and again. Tatanka-Tyotanka was so proud of his son that he gave him the ultimate gift.

"My son has earned something only I can give him," said Tatanka-Tyotanka. "I give him my name!"

And, henceforth, the boy was known as Tatanka-Tyotanka. In the language of the Sioux, Tatanka-Tyotanka means "Sitting Bull."

The Bear

One day Sitting Bull fell asleep beneath a tree by a creek. As he slept, he dreamed that an enormous bear stood above him. He dreamed that a tiny yellow bird landed beside him and told him to wake up. He opened his eyes to find himself looking into the toothy mouth of an enormous grizzly bear.

Sitting Bull wanted to run away as fast as he could. But then he saw the little bird from his dream sitting beside him. It was singing

words he could understand. "Be still," it sang to him. "Do not move!" Sitting Bull listened to his new friend. He didn't move a muscle. Soon, the bear lost interest and walked away.

*B*ravery does not always mean to go charging into danger! Sometimes it takes great courage to do nothing. To be brave does not mean to be foolish. There is a time to act, and a time to be still.

Sitting Bull, Strong Heart

Sitting Bull grew up to become one of the fastest, fiercest, and bravest men of the Hunkpapa tribe. He joined the Strong Hearts, the Hunkpapa's elite warrior society. He led many raids, fought in many battles, and became one of the most respected and feared fighters of all the Sioux tribes.

He also studied the rituals and beliefs of his people. Before going into battle, Sitting Bull would go into the hills alone and pray.

These were happy times for Sitting Bull and the Hunkpapa tribe. Millions of buffalo roamed the prairies, and the Sioux could travel when and where they wanted. Sitting Bull was made war chief of the Strong Hearts.

In the 1850s, Sitting Bull married. His wife died in childbirth, but gave him a healthy son. In 1857, Sitting Bull's son caught a fever and died. The loss of his family saddened Sitting Bull. One day a Strong Heart raiding party battled a group of Assiniboine Indians. The Assiniboines fled into the forest except for one 13-year-old boy, who stood alone with his toy bow. The Strong Hearts wanted to kill the boy, but Sitting Bull refused to let them do it. They were angry, but Sitting Bull would not back down. "The boy is my little brother," he told them. He took the boy home and made him his adopted son.

To the Sioux, it was a mark of bravery to kill one's enemies in battle. It was hard for Sitting Bull to stand against all his friends, but by sparing the boy's life and bringing him into his family, Sitting Bull showed the other Strong Hearts that *bravery* can also be used to spare a life.

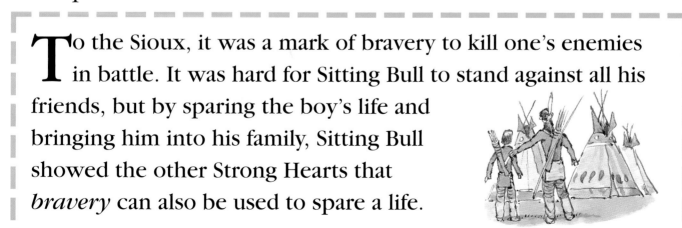

The Last of the Buffalo

During the 1860s, the Sioux saw more and more whites travel across their lands. They left behind railroad tracks, telegraph lines, and dead buffalo. Some of the settlers built their farms on Sioux hunting grounds. Professional hunters shot so many buffalo that the huge herds began to disappear.

Fights broke out between the settlers and the Indians. The U.S. government sent troops and built forts to protect the settlers. The government made treaties with the tribes, promising to stay out of Indian lands. But more and more settlers came, and the government broke one treaty after another. They wanted the Sioux to live on reservations, where they could be kept apart from the settlers.

Sitting Bull was made chief of the Hunkpapa tribe. He did not want his people to leave their homeland. But some of the other Sioux tribes agreed to try reservation life. There were few buffalo left to hunt, and the land was not good for farming. They did not get the food they were promised by the government. Many reservation Indians were going hungry. In 1862, the Santee Sioux rose up against the agents in charge of their Minnesota reservation. Over the next decade there was a series of battles between the Sioux tribes and the U.S. Army. In 1864, white soldiers attacked a peaceful Cheyenne village and killed more than 100 men, women, and children.

When Sitting Bull heard of the massacre, he was filled with anger. At the same time, he was sad, for he knew that now there could be no peace. His people would have to fight, and many would die. The western plains were a dangerous place in those years for both Indians and whites.

In 1868, the Oglala Sioux chief Red Cloud signed an important treaty at Fort Laramie. It promised the Sioux tribes all of South Dakota west of the Missouri River, an area that included the sacred lands called the Black Hills. Many Indians believed that peace had come at last, but Sitting Bull was not so sure. He became friends with Crazy Horse, war chief of the Oglala Sioux. They both believed that sooner or later the whites would find an excuse to break their treaty.

In 1874, a man with long yellow hair led a thousand soldiers into the Black Hills, where they discovered nuggets of soft, yellow-orange metal lying on the ground. The man's name was General George Custer, and the metal they discovered was gold.

RED CLOUD

GEORGE CUSTER

The Sun Dance

Once gold was discovered in the Black Hills, the government tried to buy the land from the Indians, but the Indians refused to sell. In January of 1876, the government ordered the tribes to leave the Black Hills and report to the reservations. Sitting Bull knew then that he had been right. The white government would not abide by its treaty. The soldiers would soon come to steal Indian land.

When spring came, the tribes began to gather near Sitting Bull's camp on the banks of the Rosebud River. More than 15,000 Sioux, Arapahoe, and Cheyenne camped over an area five miles long by three miles wide. Never before had all the tribes come together with a common purpose.

In June, when the moon was full, the Hunkpapa held one of their most important rituals: the Sun Dance. Sitting Bull pledged to lead his people in the Sun Dance that year. He promised to give one hundred pieces of flesh to Wakantanka, the Great Spirit. Indians from the other tribes gathered to watch the great chief perform one of the Sioux's most painful and exhausting rituals.

One hundred chunks of flesh were gouged from Sitting Bull's body. He began to dance. Blood flowed down his legs and soaked into the earth. He was in terrible pain, but he danced for many hours, waiting for a vision.

When the vision came, Sitting Bull stopped dancing. He told his people he had seen many soldiers falling from the sky. He had seen a vision of victory for his people.

A man less *brave* might have pledged fewer pieces of flesh, and could not have danced so long. Sitting Bull showed his people that he was strong and brave, and that he was not afraid to feel the pain. He showed his people he was fit to lead them in battle.

The Battle of the Little Bighorn

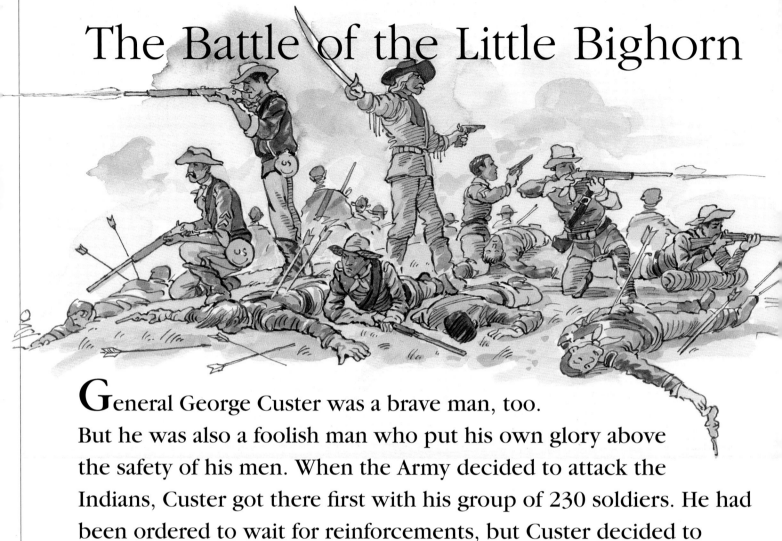

General George Custer was a brave man, too.
But he was also a foolish man who put his own glory above
the safety of his men. When the Army decided to attack the
Indians, Custer got there first with his group of 230 soldiers. He had
been ordered to wait for reinforcements, but Custer decided to
attack. If he won, he would be a great hero. He ordered his men to
attack a group of 2,000 Cheyenne and Sioux warriors at the Little
Bighorn River. Custer and every one of his men died in that battle.

Bravery means more than doing something dangerous. It is
dangerous to bang your head against a cement wall, but
that does not mean it is brave. Risking injury without a good
reason is not brave. It is foolish.

The Battle of the Little Bighorn was the great victory seen by Sitting Bull in his vision. But Sitting Bull knew that more and more white soldiers would come, thousands upon thousands of them. If the Hunkpapa stayed and fought, his people would die. So Sitting Bull led the Hunkpapa north, to Canada, where the soldiers would not follow.

But the Hunkpapa people were not happy in Canada. They were cold and hungry and they missed their homeland. In 1881, Sitting Bull led the last 187 of his people back into the United States, where he was arrested and sent to prison.

When Sitting Bull surrendered to the soldiers at the U.S. border, he gave up his rifle. He said, "I wish it to be remembered that I was the last man of my tribe to surrender my rifle."

Standing Rock

SITTING BULL

JAMES McLAUGHLIN

For two years, Sitting Bull was imprisoned at Fort Randall. When he was released from prison, he went to live on the Sioux reservation at Standing Rock, North Dakota. A man named James McLaughlin was in charge of the reservation. He was not happy to see Sitting Bull, who was still respected by his people and treated as a leader. When the government tried to take more land from the Sioux, Sitting Bull fought them with words. He had given up his rifle, but he continued to fight for his people.

James McLaughlin thought that Sitting Bull was a troublemaker. On December 15, 1890, McLaughlin sent a group of Hunkpapa policemen to arrest Sitting Bull. Sitting Bull's friends and family came to help him. A fight broke out. Shots were fired. Fourteen people died that night. One of the dead was Sitting Bull.

When Sitting Bull was born, the western prairies were covered with tall grass, blue sky, and thundering herds of buffalo. To the Hunkpapa people, the land seemed so vast and rich that there would be room for everybody—Sioux, Crow, Chippewa, and even the white settlers. When they fought, they fought for glory, for horses, or for vengeance. They did not fight for land. The land belonged to everyone.

Sixty years later, the land and its people had changed in many ways. The buffalo were gone. Railroad tracks sliced across the virgin prairie. White settlers built fences, turning traditional hunting lands into ranches and farms. Indians who had not died in battle were forced onto reservations. Many thousands of them died of starvation or disease.

Sitting Bull, once the proud leader of the Sioux nation, had died at the hands of his own people.

But one thing had not changed. Sitting Bull continued to live in the memories of his people. And so did the core values of the Sioux: wisdom, strong-heartedness, generosity, and bravery. It is these values that have sustained his people to this day.

Study Guide

Reading about famous or successful people can help us live our own lives. Sometimes we learn from their accomplishments, and sometimes we learn from their failures. Sitting Bull's life was filled with both.

1. Which of these qualities do you think are most important?

Athletic ability	Strength
Bravery	Honesty
Generosity	Perseverance
Humor	Curiosity
Health	Kindness
Patience	Fairness
Strong-heartedness	Self-confidence
Intelligence	Wisdom

Which qualities do you think were most important to Sitting Bull's people?

2. During Sitting Bull's leadership, his people lost their land and many of them died. Yet he is still considered one of their greatest leaders. Why do you think he is remembered as a great man?

3. When a 14-year-old boy Slow counted his first coup, he was honored by his people as a brave warrior. If Slow had died that day, how do you think he would be remembered?

4. Siting Bull had to make many difficult choices during his life. One of his hardest choices was to lead his people back home after living in Canada for five years, even though he knew he would be arrested. Why do you think he didn't just send his people home and stay in Canada?

Study Guide Answers

1. Different people value different qualities. A Hunkpapa warrior might say that bravery, strong-heartedness, wisdom, and generosity are most important. A scientist might prefer the qualities of intelligence, curiosity, and patience. The virtues you consider the most important say a lot about how you live your life.

2. When the white settlers began to spread west across the continent, there was little that could stop them. The whites were more numerous, they had superior weapons, and they believed that the lands were theirs for the taking. Sitting Bull and the other Indian leaders could only hope to slow them down.

   Sitting Bull gained the respect of his people through his wisdom, bravery, and generosity. He set an example, and he showed them how they could remain a proud people even under the worst conditions.

3. If Slow had died that day, his death would have been mourned by the Hunkpapa people. He would have been remembered as a brave young man who, in the heat of battle, had perhaps acted a bit foolishly. But Sitting Bull was lucky and, above all, he was skillful enough to succeed. Brave men who succeed are better remembered than brave men who die.

4. We can never know for sure what went on in Sitting Bull's mind. Perhaps he simply missed his homeland. Perhaps he did not want to be left alone. But the most likely thing is that he wanted to show his people he was not afraid. He wanted to show them he was not afraid to lead them, no matter where the road led. He wanted to show them he was a brave man.

Sitting Bull Time Line

March, 1831 Sitting Bull is born near Bullhead, South Dakota.

1845 Sitting Bull counts his first coup. His bravery earns him the name "Sitting Bull."

1856 Sitting Bull is chosen as the leader of the Strong Hearts Warrior Society

1876 General George Custer attacks Sitting Bull and others at the Little Bighorn River.

1877 Sitting Bull takes his people to Canada.

1881 Sitting Bull and his people return to the Unites States. He gives himself up to the American army and is put in jail.

1883 Sitting Bull is released from jail.

1885 Sitting Bull joins the Buffalo Bill Wild West Show and travels throughout the United States and Canada.

December 15, 1890 Sitting Bull is killed by Indian police. He is buried near Mobridge, South Dakota.